YOU'RE WHERE NOW?

Memoirs of a despatch rider

S. P. Muir

Cover photo Neil Gardose
Cover design S. P. Muir

S. P. Muir
Visit my website at www.spmuir.com

ISBN-9781790340941

For all those heroes of the London despatch scene. Ride on, brothers, ride on.

Books by S. P. Muir

Motorcycle Books:

1 – You're Where Now? Memoirs of a Despatch Rider

2 – Back This Way – Memoirs of a Despatch Rider Volume 2

Fantasy books:

The Saga of the Twins of Arl

1 – THE TALISMAN OF WRATH

2 – A WAR OF DESTINY

3 – KAMARILL: THE EARTHSOUL

INTRODUCTION

I've been asked many times to write this book. My answer has always been, "Yeah, I'll get around to it one day." Somehow though, I never seemed to have either the time or the inclination. The reason people asked me to write it is probably the flip-side of why I've procrastinated for so long. As a well-known raconteur, I've often regaled my friends and acquaintances with the more humorous anecdotes from my time as a motorcycle courier.

"You should put that in a book," they'd often say. And I wanted to; I really did. The trouble has always been that the life of despatch rider is far more than the occasional funny situation; and to write about it and not mention that would border on the criminal.

And speaking of criminal, I knew I'd have to include our frequent brushes with the boys in blue. I was also painfully aware that much of what I would need to recount would be controversial, to say the least. But in the end, I could put it off no longer.

As I write, I find myself in something of a limbo. I've just completed *A War of Destiny*, the second book in the 'Twins of Arl' trilogy, and am waiting for the rush of inspiration that will launch the third book, *Kamarill; The Earthsoul*. So rather than sit there staring at a blank page, I've decided to bite the bullet and put pen to paper, as it were.

I have to apologise to the many good and honest policemen out there. I'm sure my experiences (and those of some of my friends and colleagues) bear no comparison to the modern police force – it was after all, a different era. But although much of what I've written is anecdotal and third-hand, my own personal experiences are as accurate as I can recall them. And I've left out the worst things that resulted in the Met giving me written apologies – or even an invitation to press charges in one case!

But moving on, I have to confirm that every incident, whether humorous, tragic, or mundane, is the absolute truth and none more so than chapter twelve, *THE HAUNTED MZ OF BLACK THREE-THREE*. The only things I've changed in all the anecdotes are some of the locations, and to protect both the innocent and the not-so-innocent, the names of the people involved.

So, dear reader, read on and I hope enjoy immersing yourself in the bygone world of the eighties'

1: A FALSE START

It was an inauspicious attempt at starting a new career, to say the least. Not only was I an hour late for the interview, but unbeknown to me the excuse I used for my tardiness was the lamest, most oft used lie in the whole industry.

"I had a puncture." I said, confident that this would go down a lot better than the truth. The fact was, I'd got hopelessly lost. I'd been so busy dreaming of the huge wads of money I'd soon be earning that I hadn't even noticed that I'd crossed the river.

"Is that right?" the control room manager asked in a voice so laden with scepticism that I actually flinched.

"Yeah, I did," I replied trying to sound sincere, then added hopefully; "But I fixed it."

"And you managed to do so without even getting your hands dirty."

I stared down at the pristine, unblemished betrayal of my own hands. My mouth opened and closed in mute protestation; but there was simply no answer to the sarcastic accusation of deceit. How could there be when I was guilty as charged. I looked at the manager with the intention of asking for another chance but the look on his face said it all. With a heavy heart, I turned and walked away, resolving never to endure such humiliation again.

Of course, that was thirty-nine years ago as I write and in hindsight that should have been the end of it. If I'd had any sense, it *would* have been the end of it! I would have taken this disastrous blow to my pride as a sign from above and never entertained the idea of being a despatch rider ever again. Unfortunately, good sense has never been one of my better qualities. And so it was that just twelve months later, I set off to have another try.

2: ANOTHER TRY

Oh, the start of the Eighties; what a wonderful time that was. After the economic disasters of the seventies, for many there was a feeling of a new beginning, a time of hope. For many others of course, it became a time of deep despair as the first chill winds of 'Thatcherism' began to bite. I was to fall somewhere between the two camps. I was young, fit, and married. And before the worst of the mass unemployment had struck, although I'd lost out on my chosen career, I had a good, safe – if not the best paid – job.

At that time, I was working as an assistant caretaker at a secondary school. The man in charge would be retiring in a year or two and I was in line to take over both his job and the house that went with it. I look back now and let out a silent, frustrated scream. How could I have been so stupid!

Nevertheless, having seen the advertisement in the Motorcycle news: "No experience required, all training provided," and with a 'guaranteed' £90 a week (almost double my caretaker's wage) I was hooked. I later found out that those particular pages advertising the myriads of despatch rider jobs were known to one and all as 'The Bullshit Pages'.

I took a 'sickie' and set off for my interview, making sure that I arrived in plenty of time. The interview went quite well and I successfully managed to exaggerate my almost non-existent knowledge of London. I was pretty confident that my newly-acquired A-Z street-map book would see me through.

"You've got the job," the manager said with a smile. His face had then hardened. "But you'll have to start straight away."

So that was the catch, I was to have an immediate start "or no job". This of course was complete nonsense – all despatch companies by then were as desperate for riders as the First

World War generals were for cannon fodder! But I didn't know this and neither did any of the other poor fools who'd turned up that day.

Back at the school, my boss was understandably furious that I'd left him in the lurch; and I must confess that I did feel a fair-sized pang of guilt. But the lure of money was too strong and to get paid that money for doing what I loved more than anything else in the world meant that there was no chance I'd give up the opportunity! And the missus was all for it as well – the 'it' in question without doubt being the money. In fact, she'd even come along with me for the interview! She'd sat on the bike outside eagerly waiting to find out if we were soon to be rich.

"You won't get a reference!" my affronted boss shouted at me as I walked away after telling him the bad news.

"Don't need one," I muttered as I left the room.

The very next day I arrived at the despatch office with perfect punctuality. My excitement was almost uncontainable; and by the way the other recruits were laughing as they introduced themselves, so were they. That was the moment when I learned one of the more palatable truths about the "despatch industry". The camaraderie between the riders was probably unrivalled outside of the armed forces – not a bad analogy considering the appalling rate of attrition. With broad smiles we all introduced ourselves and ascertained the most important detail about our new associates: what bike they owned.

Mine at the time was a shiny, two-month-old Suzuki GSX250, and a real flyer it was too. It easily kept up with the air-cooled Yamaha 250 two strokes, and returned sixty to the gallon to boot! If any of us had realised the battering our pride and joys were about to receive, I think even then we might have turned away. Or perhaps not; with the money we were about to make we could easily afford a new one in a couple of months!

The manager came in to the extremely dirty and dilapidated riders' room and introduced us to one of our controllers. He was a smooth-faced, handsome chap in maybe his mid-thirties, but his countenance could best be described as severe. He eyed us all with practised contempt before sliding his backside onto the rickety table which stood under a small hatch set into one of the grime-infused walls. This led through to the hallowed sanctum of the control room; and it was through this tiny portal that the jobs would be handed out to the waiting riders.

"Right," he said with scornful disdain. "I'm going to want you all here every morning – and I mean *every* morning..." he glared at us all with utter hatred. "...by eight-thirty at the latest. You'll be given the address of your first pick-up where you'll go to their reception and *politely...*" again the glare that could strip paint. "...ask for your letter or parcel. You will then go to the nearest phone box and ring this office and tell your duty controller that you are pee-oh-bee – that's parcel on board."

"What if it's a letter?" one particularly little chap piped up with a cheeky grin. "Wouldn't that be ell-oh-bee?"

The riders all chuckled but the controller was less than amused. "If you're gonna piss around you can get out now!" he snapped angrily.

The young lad just smiled, looked at me, and winked. Little Roy and I were going to become good friends over the next few weeks.

"Won't we, like, you know, have radios?" Another rider asked. He sounding as if he'd just stubbed out a spliff on his way back from Woodstock. He was tall and bearded with long wavy hair; he was also incredibly thin and became known to one and all as 'Jesus-on-hunger-strike'. For some reason it was a nickname he relished – but then again, he was permanently stoned!

"You don't need radios!" the controller stated aggressively. "And if *we* want to contact *you*, we'll use your pagers."

I was crestfallen. This was two decades before the advent of the mobile phone (or cell phone in the USA) and the thought of instant communication had an almost Star-Trek air of adventure about it. And here we were being palmed off with a pathetic pager.

"But some of your riders have radios." I ventured.

He glared at me. "You'll have to prove yourselves before we let you anywhere near those." There was silence. Nobody dared to press him any further on that particular subject.

"Now, it doesn't matter how well you think you know London," he continued. "You're going to need a map-book. Who's got an A-Z?" *So, I hadn't needed to worry about buying it,* I thought. I joined several others in putting my hand up. He sat back against the wall and folded his arms. "Well throw it away, it's bloody useless. You want one of these." He held up a blue-coloured book about the same size as my A-Z. "This is a Nicholson's and it will be your bible. You'll have to study it at home and memorise as much as you can. The more you learn from it, the more money you'll earn."

"Do you supply them?" somebody asked.

"No!" came the firm reply. "There's a stationary shop down the road and I want you all to go and buy one as soon as we're finished here."

"What's the difference?" I asked, a bit peeved that my investment was now redundant.

"A lot. The pages in the A-Z are divided into squares. The road you want is somewhere in the square you're referred to. Most of the roads and courtyards you pick up from or deliver to are very small. You could spend ten minutes peering at the book and still not find them. Whereas this..." He held up the Nicholson's. "...is much clearer. If the reference says B6, you slide your finger down from B then across from 6, and that's your road right under your finger. You don't have to sod about searching a bloody great square. It also has some of the one-way streets marked."

Many riders nodded their heads sagely but I was damned if I was going to buy another flaming book. Everyone's heard of the A-Z but who's ever heard of a Nicholson's? If it was that good, all the tourists would use it instead!

Two weeks and many, many frustrated ten minutes' later, I bought a Nicholson's.

Soon after this we were away and it didn't take long for me to realise just how unprepared I was for my new life. I was used to the steady, plodding work-rate of a good old nine-to-five (oh all right, split shift at the school) so the relentless push to cover the workload thrust upon me by my new employer was one hell of a shock! Added to that of course, I was now self-employed and responsible for all the costs of my work. Petrol, the bike, the repairs, maintenance, clothing etc. I was also responsible for my own tax and National Insurance. And neither were there any holidays or sick pay.

I was part of what is known today as the 'gig economy'. We were paid (a pittance) for every parcel we delivered and nothing else. As I (and several of my new mates) didn't know London at all, a great deal of time was wasted just trying to find our way around. And the longer it took to deliver a parcel, the fewer parcels you could deliver; and the fewer parcels you delivered, the less money you could make. No problem of course, because we were guaranteed £90 a week.

Oh, how well I remember queuing up for my first wage packet at the end of my second week.

"What's this?" I queried angrily as I looked at the barely twenty-five quid in the little envelope. "Where's my guaranteed ninety pounds?"

"Hah!" the fearsome controller sneered. "You blew that when you were five minutes late on the first Friday."

"But...but this hardly covers my petrol and stuff."

"You should have been here on time then."

"It wasn't my fault. There'd been an accident on the Old Kent Road; it was bumper to bumper and hardly moving."

"You're on a bike; that shouldn't make any difference."

I was crestfallen. In a way he was right, of course. I was yet to learn the trick of flying down the outside (or inside, or middle of) the endless queues of London traffic. I *should* have made it on time. But to lose sixty-five quid for the sake of five minutes for crying out loud! Mind you, Roy had lost out on his minimum by *two* minutes. But then again, he didn't lose as much money as me because he'd managed to earn much, much more. He'd scooped a whole *thirty* quid! Needless to say, he was not impressed either. Still, he was a chipper little bloke and was soon smiling again. I of course, had the prospect of telling my wife; so a smile was a long way from *my* face, I can tell you!

The next week I made sure I arrived on time every day, and this being my third week in the job, I was beginning to learn the rough layout of central London. The trouble was the circuit (as the list of client companies are known) had "gone quiet." I knew I'd had fewer jobs and so had earned even less than the week before, but as I'd been scrupulously punctual, I wasn't too concerned. Once again, I opened my little envelope; once again I cried out in dismay. My 'crime' this time was not phoning in pee-uh-bee on one of my pick-ups. Technically, they were right. But since the parcel was only going a few streets and the drop-off was on the way to the nearest phone box, it seemed only logical to deliver the parcel first. Not so, apparently.

As it turned out, there were so many misdemeanours which proscribed the payment of the hallowed minimum that I don't think a single one of us rookies ever received it. Added to that, with the circuit being quiet, we newbies were way down the pecking order when it came to job allocation, so the chances of earning a decent wage were less than nil! Needless to say, I soon moved on to pastures new.

My next job from the dreaded Bullshit Pages was not actually a bad one. It was one of those sought-after despatch jobs that had two things going for it: it was PAYE (not self-employed i.e. a fixed wage with all tax paid) but best of all it came with that Holy Grail in the despatch industry, a company bike! I later learned however, that this wasn't the best way to be a despatch rider.

It was a risky job to say the least; I saw one report that listed a London motorcycle messenger as the third most dangerous job in Britain. It was only slightly safer than a test pilot and a bomb disposal expert! So, if you *are* going to risk life and limb, you might as well get good money for it.

Of course, to earn good money you need to know what you're doing, and at least I now had the opportunity to learn the craft while getting a steady – if not spectacular – wage. And my bike wasn't going to get wrecked in the process.

As I explain more in a later chapter, one of the worst things about despatching is the weather. Nothing can prepare you for the shock of what the elements can throw at you in winter. It's all very nice charging around in the summer when all you have to put up with is the occasional downpour; but come late autumn, that all changes. As it turned out, being Pay-As-You-Earn, I wasn't earning as much money as I could while staying warm and dry elsewhere. Loath as I was to admit defeat, I eventually decided to throw in the towel. With my tail somewhat between my legs, I found myself a position in retail management. Even so, my foray into the Despatch Industry wasn't a total waste of time – I had learned the basics and I now had a fair grasp of London's geography. All things that would stand me in good stead a few years later when the coming recession hit the country hard.

* * *

I was totally unprepared for it. I should have seen it coming really; the signs were definitely there but when it came, I sat there, slack-jawed and numb. I was unemployed; I was unwanted; I was on the proverbial scrap-heap. It took a day or two and a trip to the unemployment office for the depression to really take hold. How was I going to pay the mortgage? What on earth was I going to do with myself? All I could do was to make as many job applications as I could, and then hope against hope for an interview.

I think I must have sent off scores of application letters, but most didn't even get a reply. Strange how your aspirations diminish in adversity. You start off looking at things like office manager and will eventually lower your sights to the level of road sweeper. Not that I look down on road sweepers, mind. I have the utmost respect for anyone who holds down a job. In fact, I have a great deal more respect for the humble dustbin man than for those high-flying, obscene bonus-taking, millionaire parasites that disgrace our world these days.

But I digress. It got so bad that even to receive a "thank you for your application but unfortunately..." seemed like something of a triumph. A friend of mine was in a similar position. One day he turned up on his bike and announced that he'd started working as a despatch rider, and the company he worked for were desperate for riders. He even showed me

S. P. Muir

his last two wage slips and they weren't half bad.

Despite my desperation for work, I had to give the idea a great deal of thought. There were the running costs to take into account, the sheer hard graft involved, and to make things worse, I now lived about forty miles outside London. And forty miles in the rush-hour ain't no joke – even on a bike. I was almost an hour away from the action. That's an extra two hours every day I'd be putting in compared to those who lived in the London postcodes. In the end though, looming poverty made my decision for me; I was in.

The firm in question was one of the biggest, and although I still had no radio, they kept me busy enough to keep a steady – if not outstanding – amount of money coming in. As I became more and more proficient, I found that I could move on to better companies (the biggest aren't always the best) and I soon got what I'd been hoping for all along – a radio! Unfortunately, I soon learned that with this most desired of objects came frustration, anger, and frustration – yes, I know I said that twice but believe me, twice is not enough!

It's from this point that my memoirs really begin. A collection of tales that may at times have the faint aroma of bull's faeces; but I swear, they are absolutely true; at least as true as a thirty-odd-year timespan allows.

3: GEORGE WHO?

I t was summer and the work was a bit slow. It was always slow in summer – unless it was a rainy day of course, and this day was particularly warm and sunny. Summer was always slow for two reasons:

Firstly, the office wallahs who usually rang for a bike to do a 'local' delivery (Fleet Street to Cannon Street and the like) would take the opportunity for a stroll in the sunshine and take their package the three or four hundred yards themselves. With these handy (and lucrative) little runs gone, it meant that there were more riders competing for the remaining work.

Secondly: bloody students! Every year they'd crawl out of the woodwork and use their summer holiday to earn a bit of beer money. And the nice gentlemen in charge of the various despatch companies would "flood the circuit" with them. This left us poor sods who relied on the money to support our families in dire straits! Okay, we all need a good education, but putting food on your children's plates is somewhat more important than having a good time in the student's union bar. No matter how nice some of these chaps undoubtedly were (I don't recall any female students on circuit) they were less welcome than a bad smell in a lift. And we let them know it too.

Gawd, there were some thick-skinned college-types around back then. In today's world they'd be standing there, red faced and pointing at us full-timers while screaming "hate crime!" at the top of their voices! Oh, how times have changed.

"Tree-three, you're where now?" They were the words I'd been waiting to hear from my radio for about twenty-five minutes now.

"Yeah, three-three; standing by, Hanover Square."

"Roger, three-three. Ready for details?"

"Yeah Roger," I replied, pen at the ready. I took down the details then threw down my cigarette and grabbed my crash helmet. No messing around with catches or anything as time consuming as that. I'd always chosen a helmet with 'D ring' straps. You never, ever, *ever* undid it. You just loosened it enough to slip the helmet on, then a quick tug on the strap and you were away. Gloves? In the summer? Don't make me laugh. What do you want gloves for? It's not as if your hands are going to get cold now, is it? The modern day, armour-plated bikers would probably have had a nervous breakdown seeing our cavalier attitude to safety back then.

My pick-up was from an agent's office in the West End going out to an address in Radlett, Hertfordshire. A nice little earner – especially as it was a wait-and-return. That meant I'd get paid there and back. I'd also get paid for every minute over ten minutes I was kept waiting. The job turned out to be a visa application that needed filling in, signing, and then bringing back to the agent. No problem; away I went.

It was a lovely ride and I easily found the house I was looking for – and a grand house it was too. I crunched up the gravel drive and rang the bell. The door was thrown open and a woman with a lovely smiling face said, "Come on in" before I'd even had a chance to open my mouth. I looked at the lovely carpet (my memory says cream shag-pile but I could be wrong) then down at my filthy boots.

"Erm... it might be best if I wait out here," I said apologetically.

"Nonsense. In you come; we can't leave you standing on the doorstep. George!" she shouted as she led me through to the lounge. "George! The bike's here." Her calls were answered by the sound of feet pounding down stairs and almost immediately two young men came into view. One of them walked over and with a big smile held out his hand expectantly.

"There you go," I said. "I'm told I've got to wait and then take it back to the office."

"Yes, that's right; we'll try not to keep you too long. Would you like a cup of tea while you wait?"

"Only if it's not too much trouble."

"Not at all." He looked over my shoulder to where the woman was now taking a seat on the sofa. There was another woman sitting in the room as well. I'm pretty sure the young man said, "Mum?" but again, time does fog the memory a bit.

Whoever the lady was, she got to her feet and with another big smile went off to make some drinks. The two young men went over to a table and started filling in their forms while I stood awkwardly waiting for my cuppa to arrive.

"Sit down," the second woman said with a casual warmth that really put me at my ease. Even so since the furniture was, as best I can recall, white leather, I was reluctant to obey. Despatch riders' clothes were notoriously covered in grime but she didn't seem to care.

"Don't worry about it; sit down," she repeated with such encouragement that I had to obey.

I then spent twenty minutes-or-so chatting with the two ladies about what it was like to be a despatch rider. Every now and then George would chip in with a comment but for the most part, the two men concentrated on their task. The second lad was very quiet the whole time and I can't actually remember him saying one word to me. I have to say though, I didn't get any negative vibes from him; he just seemed to be the quiet sort. Maybe George's larger than life personality just overshadowed him – who knows. I came away feeling that I liked him all the same.

Eventually, they finished and George handed me back the resealed package.

"Would you mind signing for the waiting time?" I asked politely.

"Of course not. How long have you been here?"

"Twenty minutes, maybe twenty-five."

"Ah, we'll call it thirty. What did you think of our last single, by the way?"

I hope he didn't spot the confusion in my eyes as I wracked my brains trying to work out just who the hell these two good-looking lads were. After a fraction of a second that seemed to stretch on for an eternity, I knew I had only two options. Admit that I hadn't got a clue what he was talking about, or lie.

"Yeah, it was pretty good," I said enthusiastically, deciding on the latter option.

"Great, I'm glad you liked it. Our new one's just out; in fact, it'll be on Top of the Pops this Thursday." For you I-Pod, music-streaming youngsters of today, Top of the Pops was a show on the BBC that had all the top artists performing their latest hits live (usually miming very badly to them at least) or it would show one of those new-fangled video thingummies.

"Terrific," I said, hoping that he couldn't read the dishonesty in my expression.

I said my farewell's and walked back to the bike. As I went, I studied the signature on my waiting-time docket. It meant nothing to me and by the time I'd got back into London, I'd pretty much forgotten all about it. I delivered the parcel and settled down to wait for my next job.

It wasn't until later that evening when it came back to me again. "Hey, I met a pop star today," I said to the wife.

"Really?" she asked, obviously impressed. "Who?"

"Haven't got a clue," I replied, sounding almost proud of my ignorance. "It was a couple of blokes. All I know is that one was called George."

"George who?"

I wracked my brains but the surname on the man's signature was gone. The briefest glance I'd had of it, along with the many near-death experiences that were a part of every despatch rider's daily life meant it had sunk without trace. It just hadn't been important enough to take up the much-needed space in my mind.

"I don't know, I can't remember." My face then lit up. "He said they'll be on Top of the Pops this week though. We'll keep an eye out for them."

Thursday came and we sat eagerly watching, waiting for my new best friend and his musical partner to appear. And appear they did. The 'Club Tropicana' video came on. "That's them!" I cried, pointing at the telly. "That's them. It was Wham!"

So, the mysterious George in question was none other than George Michael.

"What?" I tell everyone now. "George Michael? Yeah, we were really close friends. I can remember discussing his latest record with him when I was round at his place for a cuppa. No, I'm not bullshitting; it's true; cross my heart..."

4: SINGING IN THE RAIN

Contrary to what you might think from the title, this chapter is not about inclement weather. It's about... well, you'll see.

It was one of those strange yet blissful days that seemed to happen only once in a blue moon for us despatchers. It was a lovely warm day *and I was busy.* But not the frenetic, six separate jobs at the same time, controller constantly calling your number with the dreaded, "you're where now?" type busy. No, this was a steady, one job after the other, everything slotting into place, no dead mileage, kind of busy.

Every now and then I'd find even myself with two jobs going in pretty much the same direction. So, all in all, it looked to be shaping into a nice, easy, well-paying day. I should have known that something would go wrong!

I'd just dropped off a package in Golders Green and was trying to radio in empty. However, the frustration of the dreaded radio interference had decided to raise its ugly head and no matter how I tried, I couldn't get through. I kept changing position by riding a hundred yards or so down the road but nothing seemed to help.

"Three-three, three-three." I'd call over and over.

"Three-*squawk, shh*-three; *squelch squawk screech*?"

"Say again?"

"*Squawk shh screech* now?"

"I'll get you on the phone!" I eventually cried, unable to take it anymore.

My ire was stoked even further when I then got the only clearly decipherable message in the whole conversation. "Three-three, get me on the phone, on the phone!" I could have screamed.

I knew I'd passed a phone box (remember those?) a couple of hundred yards back, so I pulled a quick U-turn and gunned the bike (a Honda 400 four) back the way I'd come.

Most riders in the business hadn't been in the game all that long. Such was the attrition rate that the average 'life-expectancy' of a London despatch rider was eighteen months. Some gave up just a few weeks after discovering the true nature of the business. Most, however, either burned out or crashed out. I was one of those rare – and much sought after – beasts that had more than two years of experience. On this occasion, that experience was my undoing.

I'd got into the habit of kicking down my side-stand, stopping the bike, and swinging my leg over to dismount all in one fluid, simultaneous movement. When you're busy, every second wasted is a second... well... *wasted.*

I arrived at the phone box, braked heavily, performed the aforementioned manoeuvre, and... disaster! My side-stand disappeared down the kerbside drain-grate. The bike toppled over onto my leg and smashed my left ankle against the kerb. It hurt. No, it *hurt*! Worst of all, I couldn't get the bloody bike off me. I was trapped!

I looked along the road and there, just twenty yards away, was a man waiting at a bus stop. He was looking at me with an expression of total apathy. There was not a glimmer of emotion. No sympathy, no amusement (it must have looked hilarious) nor even contempt. He was just *looking*!

"Can you give me a hand?" I called. "My leg's trapped and I can't shift the bike."

He studied me for a moment before he replied. "I've got a bad back," he said in a neutral, expressionless tone. He then turned his back on me with a firm finality. As far as he was concerned, the matter was closed. I looked at him in horrified amazement. He may well have had a bad back, but he could still have tried to find someone who didn't!

Salvation came when I spotted an ambulance driving along on the other side of the road. Frantically, I waved my arms around like a drowning man about to go down for the third time. Fortunately, the driver saw me and within seconds he'd turned the ambulance around and had pulled up next to me. He jumped out and along with his co-pilot, they heaved the bike upright. They looked at my rapidly swelling ankle and gently manipulated it.

"Oh, my word," I said politely. "That's a tad uncomfortable." I may well have used somewhat stronger words than that but I shall let you, dear reader, decide which ones.

"You're gonna need to go to hospital and have that x-rayed," one of them said.

"Phew," I replied. "Good job you saw me. You can get me there in no time." I couldn't believe my luck. Nor could I believe his reply.

"Sorry mate, no can do. We're going back to base and we're not allowed to pick people up without control telling us to. I can radio for another ambulance though. It should be along in about five or ten minutes."

"WHAT?" I cried incredulously. "That's mental! Won't they tell *you* to do it?"

"Afraid not. I know it's mental but those are the rules."

So he radioed in (obviously, the ambulance service needed a far better signal than I did) and ordered my hospital conveyance. Then with a cheery, "Good luck," they jumped into their ambulance and sped off.

Eventually, the new ambulance turned up and I was on my way soon after. As we drew close to the hospital, I managed to contact my controller and hurriedly told him what had happened. The swine actually laughed. The utter, utter swine laughed a lot!

At the hospital, they duly x-rayed my ankle and thankfully, I'd not done too much damage. There was something of an argument with the nurse who documented the incident though.

"As it's an RTA (road traffic accident) I'm afraid you'll get charged for the ambulance. It's about twelve pounds, I think."

Now twelve pounds in the mid-eighties was a lot of money and there was no way I was going to give up half my morning's earnings without a fight.

"How is it an RTA?" I asked incredulously. "The bike wasn't moving; it just rolled off its stand and fell on my leg."

Well, it was sort of the truth.

"It involved a vehicle so it's an RTA," she replied firmly.

"So you're actually telling me that if you were walking along the road and a parked car's handbrake failed, you'd have to pay if it rolled on to your leg? Or supposing you weren't looking where you were going and you just walked into it. It still involves a vehicle but would you be prepared to pay for that?"

Her mouth opened and closed a few times before, under my onslaught of faultless logic, she capitulated. "Very well; I'll just say that something fell on you."

"Thank You," I breathed. I knew I was going to be off work for a while and twelve quid was twelve quid – there's no sick pay for the self-employed.

Thankfully, after applying regular hot and cold compresses, my ankle was much better after just a couple of days. It was still very painful but with a pregnant wife and a two-year-old girl to feed, I couldn't stay at home any longer.

The final insult came when I walked into the office at the start of the day. I was met by a great roar of laughter from the riders and control-room staff. There was even a sarcastic round of applause. I took it all on the chin though; no doubt if it had been someone else, I'd have been doing exactly the same.

I wasn't so forgiving when I got a call on the radio later on in the day, I was riding along (I forget exactly where) when through the normal radio-chatter I heard my call sign.

"Three-three, three-three."

I fumbled with the radio until I found the key-button. "Three-three," I replied, shouting so the controller could hear me through my helmet and above the wind and road noise.

"Three-three..." I waited for the usual, "you're where now?" but instead the controller broke into song with a parody of the old musical's theme tune.

"I'm swinging in the drain,
Just swinging in the drain,
What a glorious feeling,
I've crashed it again..."

I was seriously unimpressed – especially as the stupid, ridiculous, puerile, pathetic, childish refrain was repeated every time I called in. I even had to endure it every time he had a spare moment and was bored. I decided I was going to have a serious word with him next time I went back to the office.

As it transpired, that wasn't until the next morning. I arrived at work, took a deep breath, squared my shoulders and prepared to do battle with the idiot who'd ruined my day. I marched resolutely through the door.

Half a dozen riders, two telephonists, the controller and his assistant all turned to witness my grand and dramatic entrance. Suddenly, there broke out a loud, well-rehearsed chorus of:

> *"I'm swinging in the drain,*
> *Just swinging in the drain..."*

5: THE ANGEL WITH THE PURPLE HAIR

I've already mentioned the high attrition rate in the despatch rider industry, so to have survived in it for more than eight years was something of a miracle. Okay, the greater your experience, the more aware you were of danger – and danger of *all* kinds – but I still maintain that someone or something was watching over me. Never once did I have a really serious accident but there were so many near misses, I could write a whole chapter on that. That, I feel, would begin to get a bit monotonous so I've resisted the temptation for now. Maybe if this book proves popular and enough people ask me for another volume, I'll recount some of them, but not now. There is one particular type of near miss that I will talk about though: the kind that involves the police.

Generally, I'm pretty law-abiding, but to earn a decent living there were certain rules that had to be bent beyond all recognition. The main one being – obviously – the speed limit. To us, and probably just about every biker on God's green Earth, speed limits are neither compulsory nor are they a 'target'; they are merely *advisory*. The police knew it; we knew the police knew it; and the police knew we knew that they knew it.

Oh, how they hated us. I'm not entirely sure why but they did. Maybe it was because there were so many accidents involving despatch riders; and they were the poor sods who had to clear up the mess – but more of that in a later chapter.

For whatever the reason, their intense dislike of us spawned a kind of cat-and-mouse game that went on for all the years I worked there. They'd occasionally set up speed traps on all the main despatch runs but always with limited success. They reckoned they had about ten minutes before the number of riders passing through faded away to zero. And that applied to the many checkpoints they set up as well. Ostensibly, these were safety checks to make sure that we had no faults with our bikes and that we had the right type of insurance. We riders saw them as deliberate attempts to piss us off!

Obviously, we kept a close eye out to try and spot the copper with his hand-held radar gun or the tell-tale bike in the distance with high-viz jackets clambering all over it; but the real licence-savers were the warnings over the radio.

It's actually against the law to warn other road users of the presence of the police, so to avoid prosecution there was a code. The rider who saw or was caught by either of these traps would call in.

"Three-three."

"Three-three, you called?"

"Yeah. I could swear I just saw a Klingon in the Farringdon road."

"Roger, three-three." The controller would then pass the warning on like this: "All riders;

I've had a report of Klingons in the Farringdon Road. If you're a Star Trek fan and you want to check it out, there's Klingons in the Farringdon Road – and I believe they've got ray guns."

Or:

"Three-three, you called?"

"Yeah, there's free mot's at Ludgate Circus."

"Roger, three-three. All riders, there's free mot's at Ludgate Circus. If you'd like your bike checked over, you can have it done for free at Ludgate Circus."

As I say, within minutes the number of riders passing that way would dwindle away to zero.

But that's nothing to do with my feeling of being watched over. No, there were other things. For one, there was the almost supernatural sixth sense I'd get that would 'warn' me to be careful. But even in that, I wasn't the only one. Several of my friends shared that same 'feeling' that something untoward was just ahead.

Strangest of all, however, were the odd, unexplainable 'things' that kept happening to keep me out of trouble. I shall recount one of the more notable.

It was a crisp, cold, late-autumn afternoon and the circuit was going crazy. We were inundated with work and the controller was tearing his hair out. The adrenaline was really pumping as I waited impatiently for the traffic lights to turn green. I had six deliveries to make and having had to make several detours to collect these packages, I was running late. My next delivery was FAO the editor of a certain Sunday paper's magazine supplement. This formidable woman was rightly or wrongly considered by one and all as a rude, stuck-up, bitch! As I'd been told that I had to hand the parcel to her and her alone, I knew I was in for a tongue lashing.

"Three-three, you're where now?"

My heart sank. Surely not another pick-up. At this rate nothing was going to get delivered.

"Three-three; Vernon place by Southampton Row."

"Roger, three-three; quick as you can, MOS are screaming at us."

"Roger, roger."

Oh gawd. I knew exactly what "screaming at us" meant. I was so intent on glaring at the lights, willing them to change, that I hadn't noticed the police car pulling up at the other set of lights as they turned to red. Somehow, the little sixth-sense voice in my ear had let me down.

The lights changed and I was off. I roared away from the lights with my front wheel lifting a good three foot from the tarmac. I swept round the right hander into Procter Street, my exhaust kissing the road in a shower of sparks. I flicked the bike over and the left exhaust touched down as I swung majestically into High Holborn. My mind was racing as I plotted a path to carve my way through the tight traffic I was bearing down on like a two-wheeled tsunami. I was unstoppable, I was a force of nature, I was king of the road, I was (there then came the wailing of a siren and the flashing of blue lights) nicked!

I pulled over and removed my crash helmet. The two policemen got out of their car and walked slowly and menacingly towards me. One of them pulled out his notebook and grinned sadistically.

"I'm gonna throw the book at you," he said with gleeful malice. "Speeding, driving without due care, dangerous driving. You're gonna be banned for at least a year!"

I gulped. It was bad enough that I'd lose my house and that my kids would starve – but to not ride a bike for a whole year? How in the world would I survive such cruel torment?

But then, with the thumping roar of a single cylinder four-stroke accompanied by the torturous squealing of a rear tyre, *she* appeared. In one fluid and graceful movement, she dismounted from her Honda CB250RS and swept towards us. With an elegant yet angry flick of her hand she removed her crash helmet releasing a wondrous cascade of long, purple hair. Like a diminutive, pretty, thunder-cloud of righteous wrath, she descended on the stunned policemen.

"This is an outrage!" she cried. Her voice, although thrillingly delicious and light, carried the same judicial fury as an avenging angel. "I saw everything and this man did nothing wrong. This is blatant police harassment," she added furiously as she pointed an accusing finger at the two unfortunate coppers. "I'll be a witness; I'll swear to it in court!"

With a deep and resigned sigh, the policeman shut his notebook. "You, sonny, are the luckiest man alive," he said, shaking his head in disbelief.

I swallowed hard. "I know," I said meekly.

They turned and went back to their car. Just before they climbed in, they both gave me a look of such intense hatred that if looks could indeed kill, I would have immediately burst into flames. I watched them leave then faced my heaven-sent saviour.

Her long, straight, purple hair shone in the pale autumn sunshine. Although she too was a courier, her face was clean and fresh; not blackened by the diesel-laden pollution that was smeared across the faces of all the other riders in the city. I have no idea which company she rode for; how could I notice that when I was so entranced by the beauty radiating from her perfectly proportioned features. She was more than just pretty, she was heart-achingly gorgeous.

"Here," she said pulling a pen and paper from the pocket of her leather jacket and scribbling on it. "This is my number. Phone me if you have any more problems from them – or from any other pigs for that matter."

"Thanks," I said in a pathetic whimper of a voice. "Thanks very much."

"Any time," she replied with a smile that sent my heart somersaulting around my chest. "And I mean *anytime*."

With a meaningful wink, she ran back to her bike, leapt on it and roared away. Where the hell – or heaven – did she come from? I wondered. I looked down at the scrap of paper. All I had to do was phone her one evening and find out.

With a heavy sigh, I folded it carefully and put it in my wallet, knowing that – police interference aside – it was a phone call I would never make. When all's said and done, I was after all, a married man...

6: LITTLE ROY

I've already mentioned little Roy in chapter two. He was a great little chap with an infectiously chipper sense of humour. It didn't matter how bad a day you were having, if you were fortunate enough to run into him, he couldn't help but brighten it up for you. On the last day I ever saw him, however, he was very different.

Although diminutive in stature, Roy always seemed huge, such was the size of his personality. But when he pulled up to say hello to me and another rider as we were 'standing by' in Hanover square, he seemed even smaller than his actual five-foot-three. He was quiet and diminished. He seemed to huddle down inside his waterproofs as if he were shrinking away from the world.

"What's up with him?" I asked my companion as Roy shot away on his badly repainted, white Suzuki GT250.

"Haven't you heard? He's got problems with the filth."

"How? What problems?"

My colleague folded his arms in angry indignation. "The bastards keep pulling him over for no reason. The first time he got pulled, he gave them a bit of lip – you know Roy."

"Oh yeah," I replied. Roy had a wickedly gleeful way of giving authority a bit of cheek.

"Well, they must have passed his details around and now, every time the Old Bill spot his bike, they stop him and give him the old 'free mot' treatment; and they really give him a hard time. Sometimes he's getting it two or three times a day. The SPG even stopped him once." The SPG – the 'Special Patrol Group' – had a reputation for being little more than uniformed thugs. "He was so pissed off with it all, he gave *them* some lip! He reckons they then dragged him into their van and broke his jaw."

"The bastards!" I was horrified. As hard as it was to believe – and let's face it, stories can get greatly exaggerated – it was hard to see why Roy would make it up. "Why doesn't he just change his bike; he's had that ratty old GT for ages."

"He would but he's lost so much money because of their 'attentions', he can't afford to."

The pair of us spent the next few minutes discussing the nature of the good old 'boys-in-blue' in increasingly Anglo-Saxon language. Then, through the continual squawking, interference-laden chatter of my radio, I picked out the usual, "three-three," calling me back into action.

I don't know how much time passed before the terrible news reached my ears; it could have been just weeks or it could have been months. I know I hadn't had a glimpse of Roy for a while but that hadn't really impinged on my consciousness. It wasn't until I found out about his fate that I realised he'd been absent.

"Did you hear about little Roy?" someone asked.

"No, what about him?"

"He's dead; the bloody filth murdered him."

"Murdered him!" I exclaimed. "What do you mean, murdered him?"

"Well, from what I gather, he got so pissed off that he took a swing at one of them. They gave him a good kicking and arrested him. That night he hung himself in his cell."

I don't know how true the events leading up to his death are – I never met anyone who was a first-hand witness – but I do know one indisputable fact: Roy died by hanging himself whilst in police custody. But even if the tale was exactly as told, to call it murder is far outside the bounds of credible reasoning. But whatever the veracity of the story of Roy's demise, my once high regard for the police had taken another knock – especially the Met.

It seemed that the perennial game of cat and mouse had taken a far more sinister turn; and many events after that only served to reinforce this view.

7: RAIN, SLEET, SNOW, AND ICE

I don't know where the actual statistics came from – it's possible that they were entirely made up – but the eighteen-month life expectancy of the average despatch rider was certainly accepted as fact. I *am* certain, however, that 'life expectancy' did *not* mean that the riders were actually dying. Although there were undoubtedly a lot of accidents and some were undeniably fatalities, as a breed we were *very* safe riders. It may not have looked that way but we were.

There's an apocryphal tale of Westminster Council gathering accident data in order to demonstrate what a menace we were. Their intention was to publish a report which would prove we were riding dangerously, so that then, they could ban us. When the numbers were crunched, however, the evidence was that, mile for mile, we were many times safer than your average, normal, common-or-garden variety of motorcyclist. You can't cover anywhere between thirty and fifty thousand urban miles per year without learning to protect yourself from the dangers all around you.

The main reason for the eighteen-month figure was down to the retention of man – and a very few woman – power. And the *main* reason for that was, simply put, the weather. Most – but by no means all – riders today are what we used to call "fair-weather" bikers. I make no judgement on that. If you're sitting astride a tiny machine that'll put the acceleration of a top supercar to shame; one with a top speed in excess of 160mph, you'll want the ideal conditions to enjoy said beast. But even among those riders who do brave the elements, very few will have experienced what we had to go through.

Firstly, rain. We've all ridden in the rain. Even the most fair-weather of fair-weather bikers will have been caught out at some time. To most, it's an inconvenience and nothing more than an inconvenience. It's nothing that a half-decent set of waterproofs won't keep at bay and warrants little more than a bit of temporary restraint in the right wrist. To us it was far, far more than that.

I've heard it said that many surgeons refer to motorcyclists as 'organ donors' and that they rub their hands with glee every time it rains. But it wasn't just that it turned the streets of the capital into one great skating rink. Indeed, after a good downpour had washed the slick residue from the road surface, it wasn't that bad. I certainly didn't mind that part of it too much. The main problem with rain is that it's made of water, and no matter how good your waterproofs, water has a habit of eventually working its way inside them. If you have damp clothes and are sitting in a puddle of water for even an hour or two, it's unpleasant enough. But can you imagine it for hour after hour –

sometimes eight or more – and all the while getting wetter and wetter? Nasty.

But the end of the working day was only the beginning of the next. Somehow, you've got to get your riding gear dry for tomorrow otherwise you start off with the same problem as you finished with.

Sometimes the rain could set in for several days at a time. Which brings me to another thing about water: It conducts heat away from the body many times more efficiently than air. In summer, you get cold but in winter you get *COLD!* And I'll talk about cold shortly.

Another great annoyance was trying to write down the details of your next job on an already damp docket. A docket that's being made even wetter with every second that passes while you try to scribble on it! Even if you manage to dive into an office doorway for shelter, if you don't rip your hat off first, a tiny waterfall will cascade onto your clipboard from your open visor. What on earth the office staff made of these Rorschach-style inkblots when we handed our sheets in at the end of the week, I can only guess.

And don't forget the problem of keeping your cigarettes dry! And even if your ciggies *aren't* wet, it doesn't matter how much you try to dry your hands, your fingers are so wet that your much-needed fag will be mush before it's burned halfway down.

Sleet is worse than rain because you get just as wet but you get even colder and visibility can become a problem. Sleet can also quickly turn to snow.

I can remember one time getting a job that took me out of town. I was riding along the motorway and the rain started to turn to snow. Big blobby flakes of the stuff were soon falling in an ever-thickening white curtain. Slowly, the road markings began to disappear and I knew we were in for a bad time. When I'd delivered my package, I found a phone box (I was well out of radio range) and told the controller I was going home while I still could. He was not happy about that, to say the least. With his dire threats and warnings echoing in my couldn't-give-a-toss ears, I set off on one of the most hair-raising journeys of my life.

Unless I wanted to take a huge detour, there were no major roads going in the direction of my home. I therefore had to go a good thirty-five to forty miles along a variety of very small A-roads and even some country lanes. If the motorway was becoming snow-bound what chance did I have of making it home on these much smaller ones! It's a good job I wasn't on some great big dinosaur of a muscle-bike. Oh wait, my trusty steed at that time was a CB900F, a great big dinosaur of a muscle-bike. Crap!

My clothes were already wet from a good soaking and as the temperature plunged, they began to freeze. My saturated gloves became stiff with ice and I lost all feeling in my hands and feet. Braking and changing gear became almost impossible since I had no idea where my hands and feet were, let alone what they were doing. Still, that wasn't too much of a problem since all I could do was crawl along in second gear, but the slightest touch of the brakes was becoming increasingly likely to just spit me off.

I will now make a confession on behalf of what I believe to be most of us old despatchers. Although only a very few confided in me that they'd done it, I do sincerely believe almost all are guilty: I started to whimper. Not crying, you understand, just whimpering. I wasn't even aware I was doing it at first, but once I noticed the strange, puppy-like sounds, it didn't take me long to locate the source. I'd been wet before, I'd been cold before; hell, I'd even been scared before, but this was on a whole new scale. This deepest of deep-freezes was seriously threatening my life.

I carried on as best I could, slipping and sliding alarmingly as I struggled to keep my great lump of a beast vertical and moving. Then, with a great sob of relief, I reached my home village, turned into my street and... crashed! As I was only doing around ten miles-an-hour I didn't particularly hurt myself, but the bike had smashed its alternator cover. I was in such a state of hypothermia, however, there was no way that I could pick the bike up. I tried and tried but it was hopeless. After a few minutes of pointless heaving and slipping over, I gave up. I staggered to my door, praying all the time that my wife was at home. There was not a snowball's chance in hell that I'd be able to get my gloves off, let alone find my key.

To my immense relief, within seconds of me pounding on the door she threw it open and gasped. I must have looked a real sorry state. A walking, talking – well, stammering anyway – snowman. One of my good friends, Paul, was also there and somehow, I managed to convey to him where the bike was lying. Quick as a flash, he was gone, wading through the gathering snowdrift that had once been a street like a thunderbird on a rescue mission. Somehow, he managed to get the bike upright, push it to my house, and then put it the garage. My wife raced upstairs and started running a bath before beginning to help me out of my clothes.

The first thing she removed were my gloves. My hands were a mess; frostbite was already beginning to nip at the tips of my fingers. Another hour or so and I might have been in real trouble. Slowly and carefully she stripped me naked and helped me into the warm – not hot – bath. It was agony! Slowly though, the dormant corpuscles in my bloodstream clambered wearily to their feet and began to trudge reluctantly around my body. The colour returned to my face and – thankfully – to my fingertips. After several hot drinks, a good hot meal, and numerous cigarettes, I was pretty much back to normal. It was an ordeal, however, that was seared into my psyche and one that I hoped I would never have to repeat again. Yes, I'd been covered in ice before; yes, my hands and feet had been numb before; and yes, many times I'd been soaking wet and shaking with cold. Never before though, had I been that close to succumbing to hypothermia.

We were snowed in for a couple of days but as soon as the roads were clear, I drove to a bike breaker's and secured an alternator cover for the 900. With that fitted and the weather turned to rain, I was back on the road. Little did I realise exactly what I was in for.

It was a reasonably busy day for as I've mentioned, it was always busier in the rain. Those who were single and had no financial responsibilities tended to stay at home. The rain, although fairly light at first, grew heavier and more persistent as the day wore on. By late afternoon it was not only heavy, it was turning to sleet. The temperature was dropping by the minute and it looked as though it would soon drop below freezing. Much to my controller's annoyance, I declared that I was going home early again. Ignoring his wrath, I set off for the motorway.

Soon, the sleet turned to freezing rain and the motorway became a nightmare landscape of churned-up, frozen slush. I thanked God when the rain stopped, but then the temperature nosedived into real and *serious* negative territory. Once again, my gloves froze and I'd soon lost all feeling in my hands and feet. By the time I turned into the wide country road that led to my village, I was in as bad – if not worse – a state as I'd been in a week before.

At first, I gave a silent cheer because the road was completely free of slush. In my headlight it looked as clean and clear as a sheet of glass. Unfortunately, there was a good reason for that; it was covered in a smooth and unbroken sheet of black ice.

Once again I trickled along in second gear on little more than tickover. There was a car behind me but unlike many thoughtless and inconsiderate drivers, he held way back, giving himself plenty of stopping-room for when I inevitably came a cropper.

Somehow though, I made it the mile or two to my turning without dropping the beast; but as I approached it, I was faced with a dilemma. How was I going to slow down enough to make it around the corner? Even the slightest touch of the brakes would spell disaster. My only recourse was to drop into first gear and feed the clutch in slowly and carefully. I was pretty good at this; I regularly used this method to supplement my braking in the rain. I was surprised when I found out that Rocket Ron Haslam used the same technique on the track – which is why he had a reputation of being a rain-master. So, with my hopes high, I carefully selected first and with the lightest, most delicate of touches, I slowly and skilfully fed in the clutch.

AS IF! My frozen, clodhopper feet rammed it into gear and my numb, unfelt hands dropped the clutch with all the finesse of a lumberjack attacking a tree. The rear wheel let go and the bike went down, hitting the ground like a skydiver without a parachute. The considerate car driver behind me drove not-so-considerately straight past.

This time, the crash had destroyed the engine cover on the other side of the motor; obviously I was going to have to make another trip to the breakers. What with the days off work and the expense of repairs, this was turning out to be a financially disastrous fortnight!

Once again I couldn't lift the bike, but once again Paul came to my rescue. Once again, I was undressed and helped into the warm bath and once again I suffered the agony of circulation returning to my extremities. I was physically and psychologically drawing close to the end of my tether.

Fortunately, I never again suffered *quite* this badly, but there were times when the misery of winter work – along with some of the horrors I was forced to witness – pushed me close to the edge of despair. Sometimes, that average of an eighteen-month tour of duty seemed at least twelve-months too long!

8: VOLVO!

Within the whole biking community it was once believed that Volvos were a menace. I don't know if this is still true today but such was the firmness of this belief that if you saw a Volvo, you gave it a *very* wide berth. Of course, this doctrine was anecdotal but even the motorcycle press were continually warning of this danger lurking on our streets. Then there was some research done (I think by Norwich Union but I'm probably wrong) on accident statistics involving motorbikes and the said reviled four-wheeler. On the face of it, very few were Volvo related, but on closer scrutiny, when you took into account the number of Volvos on the UK's roads, the danger was very real indeed.

There was (and probably still is) an acronym that described one particular type of accident: SMIDSY or "Sorry Mate I Didn't See You." Most accidents involving bikes happened, not at high speed, but at less than forty miles-an-hour. The car driver would pull up at a junction, have a quick look, then pull out. BANG! He'd suddenly find a bike embedded in his front offside wing and a poor hapless rider either pinned between the two or sailing gracelessly over the bonnet to land in a crumpled heap in the road. The driver's reaction – apart from asking "where the hell did he come from?" – was to repeat that time worn phrase: SMIDSY. There was even a government advertising campaign on telly and on posters warning drivers to, "Think once, think twice, think bike!" In other words: open your eyes you myopic morons! My point is, a disproportionate number of these SMIDSY incidents involved Volvos.

Which brings me to my particular coming-together with such a make of car. I'd picked up a parcel in the East-End and was on my way to somewhere west of the Square Mile. As I filtered down the outside of a long line of traffic on the

Clerkenwell Road, a big Volvo estate suddenly and without indicating tried to pull a U-turn right in front of me. I had no chance of stopping but being so experienced, I knew exactly what to do. I slammed on the back brake, locked up the rear wheel, and then threw the bike around, dropping it to the road.

This particular manoeuvre is known as 'laying it down' and allows the bike to slide tyres-first into the offending vehicle. It's a life-saver. Many of my friends survived otherwise bone-crushing smashes with little more than a few scrapes and bruises using this technique. As far as I'm aware, many of today's instructors aren't even aware of it, let alone teach it. And quite how you'd perform it on a bike with ABS I'm not sure. But I digress.

My bike and I slid only a very short distance, so close were we when Mr Volvo performed his homicidally negligent manoeuvre. Luckily, I wasn't going too fast – certainly way less than thirty – but it was enough of a thump to do sufficient damage to write my bike off. And it gave me a very nasty jarring to boot!

My immediate thought was for my urgent parcel. As I lay in the road, I managed to radio in with my position and the fact that I was down and hurt. It so happened that I was little more than a couple of hundred yards from our office, and as it was lunchtime, there were three riders in the ready room. They heard my call and as one, they leapt to their feet, rushed out of the office, and jumped on their bikes. Within seconds they arrived at the scene.

Now one of these guys – to save his blushes, let's call him Jim – was something of a beast. He was a great bloke and definitely one you'd want in your corner in a tight spot, but he was a real, wild, hard-nut. He had one hell of a temper too. The last I heard of him (again, only anecdotal) he was standing on the roof of a black-cab that had also done a blind U-turn. He was trying to batter his way in through the windscreen while screaming dire, murderous threats at the top of his voice. According to the story, he was escorted away by the plod and was never heard of again! He was an intimidating young man, to say the very least.

The little posse of riders arrived just as the Volvo driver – a Hassidic Jew complete with hat and dreadlocks – climbed out his miniature tank and stood over me. If I hadn't been in so much pain, I'd have roared with laughter at the impeccable comic timing of it all.

Volvo driver: "Of course you realise my boy, it was all your fault."

Jim (viciously smacking a fist into the palm of his other hand): "Right, which c**t done it?"

Volvo driver (seamlessly): "But on the other hand..."

The two other riders successfully restrained Jim, preventing him from stuffing the only slightly scuffed Volvo into any of its driver's orifices! Insurance details were then duly exchanged.

I now had the hassle of finding and buying a new bike – again!

9: BAD BOBBIES, GOOD BOBBIES

The antipathy between the humble despatch rider and the boys in blue ran deep – very deep in some cases. The contempt with which we were held by the average policeman ran pretty much both ways. The aforementioned "free MOT's" were probably our main bone of contention. In the police's defence however, there was probably a very good reason for their random checks. It wasn't uncommon for some riders to forget to renew their road tax – for a couple of weeks anyway; same with the MOT. "I'll do it at the weekend" would sometimes have to wait until the weekend after that if something untoward cropped up during the regular Saturday morning bike-maintenance ritual. But in *our* defence, in the main these misdemeanours were pretty rare.

Strangely, the motorcycle police – the 'Black Rats' as they liked to call themselves in the Met – were some of the worst for being belligerent if you were pulled. You'd have thought that because they too had to suffer the weather and such, they would have had a bit more sympathy; but it was actually very much the opposite. And of all these Black Rats, one was particularly reviled by one and all.

She was the only female amongst their ranks, and she was well known, even renowned, for her...erm... *thoroughness*, shall we say. If she decided to pull you over, it was wise to quickly call in and let your controller know that the 'Wicked Witch' had caught you in her evil trap. The control room would then phone the customer(s) who were waiting impatiently for their urgent package(s) to arrive. They'd have to relay the sorry fact that it would be somewhat delayed.

Whether this woman felt she had something to prove to her male colleagues, or it was simply the case that she was an outright bitch we'll never know. All I can tell you is she would go over your bike with the finest of fine-tooth combs!

Now the loud and ardent feminists of today might claim that she was hated purely and simply because she was a woman. I can categorically state that this was far from the case. I can think of around half-a-dozen female despatch riders (not counting my purple-haired angel) and they were all very highly regarded, if not revered. And I might add that they despised the Wicked Witch as much as the rest of us.

It was particularly galling for us long-term, true professional riders because our maintenance regime was incredibly strict. We *knew* our bikes were in tip-top (if slightly bodged) shape and these oft-repeated inconveniences were a waste of time.

Sometimes, though, you *could* get caught out if a bulb blew during the day or some other unforeseeable electrical or mechanical fault was to develop. I can remember one such occasion particularly clearly. Several of us had been caught up in a free-MOT trap and we were duly waiting our turn for the two plod to check our bikes over. One unfortunate rider's horn had packed in which was pointed out to him with sadistic glee.

"Oh dear, oh dear. It seems we have a problem. Your horn doesn't work. I'm afraid I'll have to write that up."

The rider grinned mischievously. "Nah, it's okay; I don't need it to work."

The copper raised a disdainful eyebrow. "You'll find the law states that you must have 'an audible means of approach' and you haven't got one."

"Yes I have."

"Where?"

The rider then took a deep breath. "OUT THE F***ING WAY!" he bellowed at the top of his voice. The policeman was unimpressed, to say the least.

Amongst the ranks of these loathed and despised, uniformed devils however, there were some absolute diamonds. They were polite and scrupulously fair; and if not exactly liked, they were nonetheless deeply respected. I'll tell you about four of them.

For some reason, they were all older than most and obviously far more experienced. Three of them were Black Rats, while the fourth I'd never seen before because he was actually Kent Constabulary (which apparently makes all the difference).

One of the Rats was well known as a good one to get tugged by. Unless you were doing something bloody daft, he tended to leave you alone. I was only stopped by him once and that was my own stupid fault. My 'radar' had short-circuited and I didn't spot him riding a few bike-lengths behind me. I'd seen a clear stretch in the traffic ahead, so with a quick flick of the wrist, I was away. I think I must have been approaching fifty when he shot past on his BMW.

"Oh, crap," I muttered to myself as I glided to a stop, dismounted, and took my crash-hat off.

"A bit heavy with the throttle there, don't you think?" he said with polite authority.

I grinned sheepishly. "Yeah, sorry about that. I saw the gap and sort of went for it."

"I realise that. There's a speed limit for a reason you know. Perhaps you can keep to it in future."

"Oh, I will," I replied earnestly.

"Alright then. Off you go; and if I catch you again, I'll throw the book at you; you understand?"

I nodded sincerely

"Okay then. Stay out of trouble."

This wonderful man then went back to his bike and roared off – clearly not heeding his own advice. I remounted and followed more sedately – a restraint that stayed with me for several days, even weeks. The result of his intervention was no less effective than if he'd subjected me to a torrent of abuse and a trip to court. The only difference was the level of respect engendered. And of course, if he *had* caught me again, I'd have considered a fine and points on my licence as fair punishment! "It's a fair cop; 'onest guv; you've caught me bang to rights."

The second of our heroes was another Rat. I can remember there'd been a bomb scare in Whitehall (we had the IRA to contend with back then) causing it to be closed off to all traffic. This had brought all approaches to parliament square to a virtual gridlock. Traffic was all being diverted over Westminster Bridge which could be pretty crowded at the best of times.

I was heading from Millbank to Covent Garden which meant going around Parliament square and up Whitehall to Trafalgar Square. It had already been a bad day. I'd been given some really difficult pickups *and* I'd been stopped by the police for no fathomable reason. Delay after delay and now this. I fought my way through the bumper-to-bumper, virtual standstill, wriggling in and out between cars and buses. I had no idea of what had caused this total snarl-up so all I could do was grit my teeth and push on as best I could. I forced my way into Parliament Square by squeezing between the traffic and the square itself. Then, when I was by Whitehall, I wriggled between two buses and hey-presto, a clear road.

With a sigh of relief, I prepared to open up the taps and fly up the empty street. Just as I took off however, it struck me as far too odd and I let the throttle go limp. As I did, a young copper – much younger than me – jumped out in front of me screaming abuse. I forget his exact words – I'm not sure that I heard all of them – but the way he stuck his red, angry face against my visor while jabbing my chest with his outstretched fingers needed no words. My seething frustration turned to outraged fury.

I jumped off my bike, ripped off my helmet and squared up to him.

"Are you F***ing stupid, sonny," he roared. "Or do you think the road's closed to everyone except you. I'll have you for disobeying a police officer."

"I've not disobeyed anyone!" I raged. "How the hell was I supposed to see what was going on from behind those buses!"

"Don't give me that. It's bloody obvious what's going on."

"It is if you're f***ing psychic! But I left my sodding crystal ball at home."

"Don't you swear at me you little shit!"

"Why not, you're a f***ing arsehole."

We were now nose to nose and this arrogant, still-wet-behind-the-ears, youngster was about to arrest me. But then another copper, one of my four good bobbies who was directing traffic twenty yards away, left his bike and came running over.

He was much older than either the belligerent young copper or me. His bearded face, normally open and friendly, was now frowning and serious. He forced himself between us and pushed, not me, but his colleague away.

"Alright, alright; what's going on?"

"This little shit disobeyed the roadblock *and* he's been using offensive language and threatening behaviour. I'm about to arrest him."

The good cop turned to me. "Well?" he asked calmly.

"Yeah, I made a mistake. I squeezed between those buses over there and started up the road. As soon as I realised what I'd done I stopped. But then this stupid prat jumps on me and starts pushing me around and reading me the riot act!"

The youngster lost it and tried to push past the older man. His face was now puce with fury. I'm guessing this was the first time anyone had failed to be intimidated by his all-too-new uniform. His elder and better had no difficulty in restraining him, however. The bearded hero nodded back towards the gridlocked melee of the square.

"Go on, off you go," he said placidly.

With a grunt of thanks and a final glare at my antagonist, I climbed aboard my bike and turned it around. Just as I was about to re-enter the chaos I glanced into my mirror. I couldn't help smiling at the sight of the old Black Rat giving his terrified junior the roasting of his life. Justice has been served, I thought.

You might be led to believe that I only consider the lenient, off-you-go-then, type policemen (and women) to be good bobbies. Not so; it's the *attitude* of the officer that counts as I shall show next.

I was hurrying along one particular Kent road, rushing back to the city as quickly and as safely as I could. Unnoticed, the speed limit on one stretch of road had changed. I wasn't exactly entering a built-up area but it definitely required a bit of a reduction in speed. Therefore, I eased back a little from my safe but illegal seventy. Suddenly, about a hundred yards ahead, a uniformed figure stepped out into the road and signalled for me to stop. I duly pulled up beside him and performed the usual polite, dismount-helmet-off routine.

"That's a nice bike you've got there," he said admiringly. "It's big for a two-fifty isn't it."

My GSX was getting a bit long in the tooth now and had been relegated to 'spare bike' status, but it was still in pretty outstanding condition.

"Yeah, it's a fair size – not as big as those Superdream monstrosities though."

The copper then bent down and gave the bike as thorough a going over as a 'free MOT' but he did it in a way that gave the impression he was admiring its design. The way he went about it inspired pride in my steed, not anger at the copper. When he stood up again, we had a little chat about the pitfalls of riding in London etc. It was all very disarming. Then:

"I suppose you're wondering why I stopped you."

"It had crossed my mind," I laughed.

"Well you see that car down there?" He pointed to a car parked a hundred yards or so back the way I'd just come.

"Yeah," I replied warily.

"I'm afraid that's a radar trap and it just clocked you at fifty-six miles-an-hour. Unfortunately, this is a thirty limit so I'm going to have to book you for it. I'm really sorry about that."

"Oh, that's okay – you're only doing your job I suppose." I felt deep disappointment but no real animosity.

When we'd finished going through the necessary legalities, I got back on my bike and prepared to set off.

"You take care now," he said sincerely.

"I will," I called. "Thanks."

It was only later in the day that I realised the irony of thanking the man who'd just cost me a hefty fine and put three points on my licence to boot. As I say, attitude.

I've saved the best example until last. I was returning to the 'middle' from a Lewisham drop. Everything had come to a complete stop – and I mean a *complete* stop! There'd been some kind of terrible incident (I can't for the life of me remember what) and unusually, everything was snarled up in *both* directions. The usual technique of filtering down the outside of the traffic was made almost impossible by the total foul-up.

Heroically, I battered my way forward until I came upon the unmistakable shape of a white, orange-striped, massively faired, police BMW. It was parked in the middle of the road and pointed in the same direction of travel as myself. Its rider was standing beside it and staring fixedly over the two bikes (more despatch riders) who were waiting patiently behind it. I managed to stop behind these and copied them by switching off my engine. I recognised the Rat as one of the genuine 'good eggs' so I wasn't worried about any untoward shenanigans he might be about to perform. I was, however, deeply intrigued about why he was gazing so intently behind us.

Slowly, the number of riders – almost entirely made up of my colleagues – began to grow until after about ten minutes or so, there must have been more than twenty of us. To my surprise, the bearded bike cop then began counting us. Obviously satisfied with our numbers, he nodded to himself and mounted his bike. He turned around and waved his hand in several circles to indicate that we should all start our engines. The air was rent by the sudden lusty roar of a couple of dozen bikes. Facing forward again, he raised his arm high into the air, then threw his hand straight ahead. We all then began to move, following our leader like rats following the pied piper.

With his 'blues and twos' clearing a path, he led his unlikely convoy all the way through to where the snarl-up ended and the road cleared. He then pulled aside and waved us all past. As we sped by, every one of us tooted our horns and waved to him in gratitude. He nodded his acknowledgement to every single rider and the smile on his face warmed my heart for the rest of the day.

10: EXCUSES, EXCUSES

The control room of a courier company was an odd place. Most of them – in the smaller companies anyway – were set out with varying numbers of telephonists sitting at a central desk. Either at one end of this desk or at one close by sat the most important man in the whole company: the controller.

A good controller could keep the movements of a dozen different bikes in his head at one time. When new jobs came in, he would arrange the dockets on his desk ready for the job details to be relayed to the appropriate rider. Most had a particular style of working, a method of allocation that was unique to them. It wasn't unusual for an experienced rider to follow one particular controller from company to company. If there was a mutual understanding, it was a partnership that benefitted them both. These men – these demigods – were worth their weight in gold – which was pretty much what the *really* good ones were paid.

When a circuit was very quiet, the control room would be filled with boredom and idle chatter. The telephonists, mostly but not always girls, would sometimes file old dockets away or check whether customer details were up to date. But most of the time, there was simply nothing for them to do. Some would paint their nails, others would read a book, while others simply chatted. When it was busy, however, it was a completely different story.

The phones would ring every couple of minutes – every few seconds when things got really crazy. The telephonists would then truly have their work cut out. Most of the calls they handled were simply more customers booking a bike. If the client wanted a package picked up out of town and brought back to them, they tended to ask how long it would take for a rider to get there. The telephonist would then shout over to the controller, something like, "Hounslow to west-one; how long?" The controller would then study 'the board' for a few seconds while mentally picturing where his bikes were and where they were going to end up. If he had a rider coming empty that way or at least passing close by, he would shout back his estimate. If it was an awkward one and nobody was going anywhere near it, he'd ask who the customer was. If it was a big account, he would re-juggle the riders' movements in his head, working out how best to re-route one of them. For these valued clients he'd do his absolute best to make a prompt collection. If, however, it was a customer that rarely used us or even one of the few cash jobs (people who ordered a bike so rarely that they had no account and paid the rider with real money) he'd give a longer estimate and basically put the job out of his mind. Eventually someone would be going that way.

There was another type of call that mostly happened at these times and it was a call that was dreaded the most.

Almost all customers believed that when they booked a bike, the controller called the next free rider on the radio, that rider went straight to the collection and then he went straight to the delivery address. In the slack, student-flooded circuit of summer, this was usually true, but when it was busy, *never*!

Obviously, the bikes always started the morning 'empty'. They would then either go to the office and wait for their first job or they would park up at their favourite spot. This would tend to be somewhere that was handy for as many different customers as possible. The nearer you were to a pick-up, the more chance you had of being chosen for that job. When the day got going, the rider would be given more and more jobs; and not just when he was 'empty'.

I personally found that there was a work-load level that was ideal. I'd be riding along, heading for the next drop with two or three packages on board. Then would come the "three-three, three-three," from the radio nestling at my left breast. It was slung on its strap across my shoulders, shrouded in its waterproof, bag-like cover.

"Three-three."

"Three, three; you're where now?"

"Theobald's going TCR, Great Portland, and Hanover," or some such answer. In plain-speak that would mean "I am at present on the Theobald road on my way to a delivery in Tottenham Court Road. After I've delivered there, I have two more deliveries. First, I shall go to Great Portland Street after which I shall be empty in Hanover Square."

Details would then follow which hopefully, would be on the way to one of these destinations. It was a lovely, steady, don't-have-to-think-too-hard, lucrative kind of way of working. Everybody liked it; the riders, the controller, the telephonists, and of course, the customers. But when it got really busy; that's when the complaints started coming in thick and fast.

In at least two of the companies I worked for, there was a list on the wall – the excuse board. These 'reasons' for the delay in either the collection or delivery of the package contained things like, "Accident," or "Puncture." Being stopped by the police was even up there. The girls would share a notepad on which they'd scribble what excuse they'd used for which customer. Sometimes a rider would be so waylaid by new pickups that the customer would ring several times. The telephonist would then cross off which excuse they'd used last time and give the irate caller a new one. The controller would often pass on to the rider the list of catastrophes that had befallen him so he could look suitably frustrated when he eventually arrived.

"Three-three, when you get to Vogue Magazine, you got stuck in a lift at your last drop, roger?"

"Rodger, Rodger, 'odge." The third "Rodger was always abbreviated like that. Some riders could manage a string of 'Rodgers' but I could only ever manage three. It was a matter of pride as to how many you could say; just why we felt the need I'll never know, but that's just how it was.

I can remember one particular day when I heard an angry customer given the best excuse ever. The Post Office was on strike and everyone-and-their-dog wanted a bike. People who had never used us before were phoning for one. For some reason I was in the office acting as co-ordinator. This meant I was the liaison between all the telephonists and the controller. It was my job to try and take some of the pressure off everyone – particularly the man 'on the box' as the controller was called. Occasionally, I even took one of the calls. It was in this role that I witnessed the chaos there first hand.

The excuse list should have burst into flames, so hard was it being worked. It made sense to prioritise the jobs by the value of the customer; the more often they used us, the higher up the pecking order they were in collection and delivery. Cash customers were at the bottom of the pile while the 'never-used-us-before' people were sub-basement!

On the day in question, one of the latter was being particularly persistent and increasingly belligerent. It certainly didn't take long for the telephonists to run out of our pre-set excuses. Eventually, the poor girl who took the final call was on the end of an exasperated, furious tirade as the customer vented their spleen. Red-faced, her mouth opened and closed as she tried to get a word in edgeways. She looked over at the control room manager with desperate pleading in her eyes. Angrily, he snatched the receiver from her and shouted that forever-remembered excuse.

"Look, he's had a puncture in a lift and his hovercraft is full of eels; SO F**K OFF!"

For a second or two, all went quiet as everyone stared at him in shocked admiration. Then as if by some kind of signal, the loud, frenetic chaos resumed.

11: BLOOD, SWEAT, AND FEARS

One of the worst things about spending all day – day after day – riding around London was witnessing the frequent and sometimes terrible accidents. Not really surprising considering the weight of traffic, U-turning black cabs, frustrated white-van-men, and most common of all – lemmings. The latter were what we'd labelled the pedestrians who seemed so keen to emulate those furry little Scandinavian rodents who have a propensity to follow each other over a cliff. If one pedestrian stepped off the pavement, all the others would blindly follow them!

There was one such occasion when one of these suicidal creatures walked out in front of a bike on our circuit. He swerved to miss her and hit a bus coming the other way head on. He was killed outright while the woman simply disappeared into the crowd. She probably had far more important things to attend to. Why else was she in such a hurry that she ran out into the path of an approaching motorcycle.

The news of the tragedy was relayed over the air for every one of us to hear. The controller finished off by giving us all a chilling instruction.

"So, if a lemming jumps out in front of you, run them down! Better them than you; and at least they won't be able to run away!" As cold-blooded as it sounded, we all resolved to do just that. Who knows, it might just be the silly bitch who'd killed our friend we were running down.

Most of the accidents I saw were very minor – some even laughable – but there were those few that will stay with me for the rest of my life. Two of these are among the many nightmares that wake me up screaming and leave me wide eyed and sweating in terror.

I won't go into too much detail in case any of the poor unfortunate relatives of those killed should read this book. I won't even name the streets because you never know...

You would have thought that with these events being seared into my brain, I would remember every little detail; but for some strange reason, a lot of it is unclear. It's as if those parts of the picture are so unimportant that my memory has clouded them in a thick mist. A sadistic thing for my brain to do as it highlights the worst of the horrors in stark relief.

The first incident happened when I was on one of London's main through-roads. At this point it's a six lane 'highway' that was more often than not bumper to bumper. I was a few car-lengths behind a young lad on what I think was a small trail bike. He was obviously new to the game but in spite of that lack of experience, he wasn't doing a bad job of carving a speedy path through the thick traffic. Unfortunately, despite his more than adequate riding skills, he hadn't yet developed his sixth sense – his radar.

I saw it coming even as he approached the danger zone. Just a feeling, but one so strong I couldn't help shouting, "Watch out!" Not that he could hear me of course – he was too far away.

Nothing had yet happened, so other than that 'feeling' there was no visible danger for the poor boy to see. But the way that taxi had moved ever-so-slightly to the right and then to the left; the fact that he'd just passed on the inside of the big lorry that was now picking up speed in the third lane; the way that the car in front of the lorry was accelerating a tad more quickly creating a space just in front of the taxi that was in the second lane. To me, it all just 'smelled' wrong.

I can't remember exactly how it occurred, but I'm guessing it happened this way. Just as the young lad was going through, the taxi started to swerve right to fill the space that was appearing in the third lane. The rider tried to swerve around the taxi, clipped the lorry and lost control. I can't be certain because everything from shouting my warning to standing next to the mangled, bleeding body lying half under the lorry is a blank. I don't even remember if I gave a statement – perhaps I just got back on my bike and rode off. The poor kid was clearly brown-bread and there was nothing to be done other than watch all the blood spreading across the road in a way that in my nightmares resembled a scarlet tsunami. I can remember wondering how the human body could contain so much of it. Even to write about it causes me to shudder.

The second incident involved a pushbike. I have to mention my antipathy for these pests, as they were then considered. It's the way that so many of them seemed to think it fine to ignore every rule of the road in the book. Yet at the same time would howl abuse at even the slightest infraction by any other legitimate road user.

In defence of the pedal-pushing road-warriors though, I will admit that they are extremely vulnerable, and most are perfectly law-abiding. The man at the centre of this tale gave no impression of being one of the former arseholes; his only crime was abject stupidity. And that crime carried a terrifyingly cruel death penalty.

I was behind a big bin-lorry and as we approached the traffic lights, I noticed the lorry's left-hand indicator start to flash. He was obviously going to turn left. We stopped and I decided to position myself on the outside of the lorry ready to shoot smartly away when the lights turned green. Just as I began my manoeuvre, however, I spotted the push-biker squeeze – and I mean *squeeze* – between the kerb and the bin-wagon. The inevitable happened. The lights changed; the lorry moved; the man shouted; his shout turned to a scream; a scream that was suddenly and sharply cut off.

Once again, there was a mangled body. Once again, there was blood – although thankfully not as much as the first time. Once again, my mind seized hold of the sight to be used to torture me with later in life.

Although I had several accidents myself, I only ever had two trips in an ambulance and even then, I wasn't too badly hurt. I was very lucky. And the more accidents I witnessed, the more I realised just how lucky I was. As the years rolled by though, the thought that I was riding my luck harder and harder every day made it harder and harder to leave the house every morning. And I wasn't the only one who felt like that.

One of my closest friends in the business – I'll call him Nigel – actually broke down in tears one day. Although the poor bloke had no family to support, he still had his rent, his bills, and a big bank loan to pay. He had no option but to keep on keeping on. Even so, his days off sick were getting more and more plentiful by the month. Pretty soon he was falling behind with everything. I helped him where I could, and even though she seemed incapable of seeing *my* pain, my wife was very sympathetic to *his* plight.

Fortunately for Nigel, his estranged Canadian father invited him to go and live with him there. Nigel came over and asked our advice on what he should do. "Go!" we both cried in unison. A few weeks later, he did. I have no idea how it turned out for him, but I pray that this tortured, good man found some well-deserved peace at last. God bless you 'Nigel'. I hope you don't suffer from the same nightmares as I do; the same dreams of blood, sweat, and fears.

12: THE HAUNTED MZ OF BLACK THREE-THREE

Of all the tales I have to tell – and only a very few are related in this book – the haunted MZ is the strangest and most difficult to believe. I've often told people the story and I don't think anyone has ever believed me. And I bet those who witnessed it all first-hand aren't believed when they tell their friends what they saw that spine-tingling summer. But whether you believe it or not, every single word of this is true

It was in the late 80s and at the time, my faithful workhorse was a Suzuki GSX400. The poor thing had done well over seventy thousand miles and was getting a bit tired. When the alternator stator burnt out for the second time – a weakness of all Suzuki's of the eighties – my boss hired a sweet, six-month-old, black MZ ETZ250 for me.

I'd owned an old Supa 5 MZ before and really liked it, but the ETZ was a revelation. It had the same silky-smooth big single with its amazingly torquey engine, but it also had an oil pump instead of the messy pre-mix. Best of all though, instead of that rather inefficient front drum, it had a large front disc with – wait for it – a BREMBO calliper! I kid you not! Honestly, on such a tiny lightweight, at anything less than a thousand miles-an-hour, that Brembo was bloody lethal. Talk about *over*-braked.

Anyway, I fell in love with it. After several happy days, I asked the bike shop I was renting it from if I could buy it. They gave it some thought and after a few hours got back to me and said okay. My boss handed the money over straight away, and I paid it back over the next couple of weeks. As soon as the damned bike was mine, however, the trouble started. The evil spirit possessing the accursed thing obviously took exception to the audacity of my purchase.

The very first job the next day (Friday) I went to the pick-up, collected the parcel, and went back out to the bike. Kick-kick-kick-kick. Nothing. Absolutely bloody nothing! In the end I had no choice but to call in over the radio and say that I'd broken down. Another rider was given the details and duly arrived to take the parcel from me. As you no doubt remember, being self-employed, even though we all worked for one company or another, we only got paid for each package delivered. The gig economy was alive and kicking even then. So of course, I earned zero on that job.

The rescuing rider arrived and after a pitiless, good laugh at my misfortune, he took off with my parcel. Sadly, I watched him go, had a cigarette, and then checked the bike over. Everything seemed fine. The plug was sparking okay and there was definitely fuel getting through, so why wouldn't it start? I decided to give it another go. Would you believe it? First kick and brrring-ding-ding-ding... Yep it fired straight up.

"Black three-three, three-three," I said into the radio. At that particular company there were at least three other firms using the same radio channel which could have got confusing. So to avoid mix-ups, we had to prefix our call signs with the word 'black'.

"Black three-three?"

"Yeah, three-three, mobile again."

I was given a new pick-up and guess what? Same thing. Kick...kick...kick.

"Black three-three; broken down." And once again it started up as soon as the parcel was away on another bike. It was the same flaming thing all day. By knocking off time, all that I'd earned was a cancellation fee (which is where the rider arrives and they say that they don't need him after all) and a great deal of frustration.

To rub salt into the wound, it ran beautifully all the way home. I spent that evening in the garage going over it with a fine-tooth comb. I checked everything, but could find nothing wrong. Even so, to be on the safe side I bought a new coil, condenser, points, and sparkplug. Good job spares were cheap on the MZs.

Monday came, and it went like a little rocket all the way to work. At one point I gave it full throttle and was clocked at 87mph by a guy on a GPZ550. The poor bloke was apoplectic with shocked amazement. At the first set of traffic lights he demanded to know what I'd done to tune it. I just smiled to myself. I had no idea quite why this piece of East German kit was so quick but I wasn't going to complain about it.

But once I started work, the same thing happened. Every time I picked up a parcel, it wouldn't start. As soon as the new rider had disappeared, gliding away over the horizon, brrring-ding-ding-ding. Away it would go.

Then adding to my woes – and just to confirm that this thing really was demonic – I was sitting at a set of traffic lights when the bike went 'pop' and then carried on ticking over. I glanced at the tacho, but it said no revs. I blipped the throttle and sure enough, brrring-ding-ding-ding.

Bugger, I thought. Now the tacho cable's snapped. The lights changed and I pulled away...*in reverse*! Honestly, the damned engine was running backwards! I turned it off and restarted it and away it went in the right direction.

Twice more it did this. Nobody would believe me until it did it right outside our office. Everyone rushed out to witness this incredible sight and promptly fell about laughing. That was it. I parked it up and borrowed a bike for the rest of the day.

The last job of the day was a regular four-hundred-yard jaunt from Ludgate Hill to Cannon Street. My good friend, black four-two who I always rode home with when I could, had the privilege of this cushy job that evening; but he kindly offered it to me. I'd handed back the borrowed bike and was obviously taking the MZ home. With my friend following behind me we set off. The bike ran fine to Ludgate Hill – better than fine, it was great. I then went in, collected the parcel, came out again, and...problems.

Okay it started, but for the whole four-hundred-yards it coughed and spluttered and wouldn't go over 25mph. I made the delivery and hey presto, when I restarted it, the evil, black-painted, demonic bitch ran perfectly.

Pissed off, I wrung the bloody thing's neck all the way home, maintaining a steady 80-85 all the way. I sold it to a bike shop in Gillingham from where one of four-two's friends bought it. And to rub *even more* salt into the wound, it behaved perfectly the whole time he had it.

And so, the Legend of the Haunted MZ was born. I wrote the following poem which was then printed off and hung on the wall of the control room.

THE LEGEND OF THE HAUNTED MZ

The devil came down to Clerkenwell,
To find a soul he'd like,
When he spied a despatch rider,
On an old and clapped out bike.

So he said to this young rider,
"Please son, won't you tell to me,
What call sign do you go by?"
The reply was "Black three-three."

So the devil said, "Boy I've seen you ride,

And you go at a hell of a lick,
But if you don't mind me saying, son,
Your bike looks kind of sick,

But as I'm in a good mood,
And unlikely as it seems,
If you can beat me in a race,
You can have the bike of your dreams."

Well, three-three frowned and said "Okay,
If I win that sounds just fine,
But what will happen if I lose?"
The reply: "Your soul is mine!"

But three-three signed his name in blood,
Cos he really knew no fear,
At least until the moment,
The devil's ride did appear.

It was a fiery beast from hell,
With flames instead of feet,
And the devil leapt upon its back,
And scorched off down the street!

But three-three followed close behind,

His cycle belching smoke,
Well, the poor thing was quite past it,
And had lost most of its poke.

But three-three was a master,
At slicing through the town,
As he went round Hyde Park Corner,
He got his left knee down.

Then into Piccadilly,
Scattered lemmings left and right,
Dodged inattentive white van men,
And kept the devil in sight.

He took the lead in Regent Street,
But his bike had got too hot,
And with a loud explosive backfire,
It dropped onto one pot.

The devil scorched on past him,
And cos he was a swine,
He laughed an evil laugh and said,
"Your foolish soul is mine!"

But the angels handed victory,

To three-three on a plate,
When a taxi pulled a yewie and said:
"Sorry, didn't see you mate!"

Three-three limped on past the crash,
And crossed the finish line.
He cried, "I beat you devil,
Now a dream-bike will be mine!"

The devil? A good loser?
That surely is absurd!
But the contract was in red and white,
So he had to keep his word.

But all kinds of twisted nightmares,
Writhed in three-three's head,
And the motor cycle in those dreams,
Was a haunted, black, MZ.

13: FASHION SHOOT

Of all the jobs you could be given, fashion shoots were among most riders' favourites. They usually involved a fair bit of waiting time which, of course, we were paid for. This remuneration wasn't exactly generous (at least not with most companies) but in the all-too-frequent slack periods, it was far more profitable than sitting on stand-by earning precisely nothing. And *that* entailed worrying about how you were going to justify your meagre wage packet to the housewife at home. The flip-side of the coin was when it was busy. Your workmates were charging around making a mint while you were standing there, waiting for some arty-farty photographer to finally satisfy some over-critical designer. And *that* entailed worrying about how you were going to justify...oh, you get the picture.

Whether slack or busy, winter or summer, a lot of these shoots did have one feature that all the male, straight riders appreciated – the models. I hadn't realised just how uninhibited these girls had to be. They'd readily strip off down to their undies (which was sometimes just their briefs) while they changed into the next outfit to be photographed.

Now, in this modern, me-too age in which we now live, it isn't acceptable for a young, virile, dirt-encrusted man to be leering at... I mean, casting an admiring eye over semi-naked and extremely pretty young women. In my defence, I did often find it a little embarrassing. Many times I averted my red-faced gaze; but even so, I couldn't help allowing the occasional Sid James-type "phwoar" from entering my mind.

However, the particular fashion shoot I want to relate to you here, dear reader, was of a far, far stranger – possibly unique – kind.

It was high summer and I was on stand-by in Soho's Golden Square. I was sitting (lying actually) on my CB900 waiting for a job to eventually come my way when a couple of vans pulled up and out jumped what was obviously the usual fashion-shoot entourage. Curious, I sat up and watched the goings-on. Although I'd seen the whole thing many times in a studio setting, it seemed extremely odd to see it all in such an unusual location. There was only one model and she was soon performing all the customary poses that showed off the latest clothes hanging on her stick-thin figure.

Suddenly, the photographer and a woman who was obviously in charge of the whole thing, put their heads together and kept glancing in my direction. Eventually, the dude with the camera strolled over to me and explained what was going on.

"Sorry to bother you," he said with a politeness I'd not heard from his ilk before. "But we're doing this fashion shoot for Vogue Magazine."

"Very nice," I replied, wondering where this was going.

"Yes, it is. But; well; what we're wondering is, if you wouldn't mind, could we possibly use your bike?"

"Erm...how do you mean?" I asked cautiously. There was no way I was going to let *anyone* ride my bike – no matter who the photographs were for.

"Well, could we have her...you know... sitting on it?"

"Ah; of course. No problem at all."

I then spent an amused five minutes watching this tall, pretty, and amazingly-dressed model sit, lay, and generally drape herself all over my dirty, somewhat ratty-looking 900. But no matter what poses she struck, the man with the camera was dissatisfied. Eventually, he approached me again.

"I don't suppose you could take her for a spin around the Square, could you? It'd make a fantastic image – you know, the smart, modern working girl grabbing a lift to work with a despatch rider."

I shook my head. "Nah, I haven't got a spare lid. If the old bill spotted us, we'd both get done. I could even get points on my licence."

"Look, don't worry about that. If the police should come, we'll smooth it over. They're usually pretty...erm...'amenable' in this type of situation."

I gave it a moment's thought. I have to say, the thought of that slim, pretty young thing, clinging tightly to my waist and pressing her body against me never even entered my mind. But still, the law was the law. No way was I going to jeopardise my licence for the sake of a glamourous, beautiful...

Two minutes later, I was prowling round and around Golden Square with a gorgeous, helmetless girl clinging tightly on to me as she sat delicately side-saddle on the back of my well-used bike. Every time we passed the photographer, his camera began clicking away on auto like a German machine-gunner at the Somme. After a disappointingly short time, he waved us in and the girl got off. She then spoke to me for the first time.

"Thank you," she breathed, giving me a smile that could set the hardest heart aflame from a hundred yards. She looked as though she'd enjoyed the experience almost as much as I had.

"No problem," I replied, hoping I sounded sophisticated enough to move in her elevated social circle. "Anytime."

She turned her back and walked away in a manner that spoke volumes about my lack of success on that score.

"Brilliant!" the photographer gushed. "That was just what we wanted. Thanks very much. It'll be in the next edition of Vogue."

"No it won't," the boss woman corrected as she arrived at his side. "The next one has already been set. It'll be in the one after that."

"That's great," I said. "I'll make sure I buy a copy."

The woman studied me for a moment then shook her head. "No, I've a better idea. When that edition hits the shelves, call into the reception and tell them you're the rider in that month's feature. We'll give you a free copy and we'll also give you some of the negatives as a memento. I'm sure there'll be plenty to spare."

And that's exactly what happened. Thankfully, my wife wasn't the jealous type, and me having a lovely model draped all over me didn't faze her at all. She was actually quite excited that her husband was going to be famous – for one month in my life at least. Six or seven weeks later, I duly turned up at the Vogue Magazine reception in Hanover Square. I told the confused girl at the desk who I was.

As with many of these establishments, there was a post room that we humble couriers were under strict instructions to use. This prim, attractive, and very stuck-up girl seemed most put out that a scruffy, grime-smeared despatch rider had the affront to enter the hallowed ground of her reception area. But I eventually persuaded her to phone somebody more senior. Much to the girl on the desk's disgust, I was then escorted with great respect to some kind of production office. I was given my mementos and they became a treasured reminder of one of the few really worthy days of that tiresome era in my life.

I wish I still had them, I really do. They would be proof that this particular anecdote is true. I'm sure that when I relate this experience – and many others – to my friends and acquaintances, they think to themselves; "Boy, this man's full of first class, grade-A, bullshit!"

Unfortunately, as with many other things, they've disappeared. Just one of the many dire consequences of divorce. I ascribe no blame for their mysterious vanishing; I may well have misplaced them myself – it's more than likely that I did. Even if I could find a copy of that issue it would be something. I've tried to locate a back-copy on ebay but to no avail. It would, of course, help if I knew exactly what issue I was looking for. I think it must have been a September or perhaps even a November; but which year? It has to be somewhere between '88 and '91 but who knows? It was a long time ago.

I doubt that anyone reading this book would be the type to subscribe to Vogue, but if by any chance someone, somewhere does; and if that person is old enough to have read that particular issue, that man on the big red and white Honda, was me!

14: A FLY IN THE EYE IS WORTH A BIKE IN THE BUSH

Boy, it was hot! Damned hot! A friend had a thermometer on his bike and when he was squeezing between the buses, it went off the scale! I tell you, if we'd been wearing all that Kevlar, armour-plated, mustn't-graze-your-knee type of clothing the bike instructors insist you wear today, we'd have died from heat-stroke!

A lot of riders were hooning around in shorts and tee-shirts, but I wasn't quite that extreme. I still wore my ubiquitous Rukka jacket, but I'd pulled the sleeves up to expose my forearms.

Protective footwear consisted of a pair of trainers whilst my gloves had lived undisturbed in my top-box for a couple of weeks. For once we were glad the circuits were quiet for it gave us all a chance for a bit of sunbathing at the various stand-by spots.

Late one Friday morning, I was given a multi-drop job. These weren't usually popular because they weren't very well paid for the amount of time they took to finish. This one, however, was a peach. Pick up in the West-End and deliver to six addresses from Chiswick all the way down to Guildford. A lovely summer's day ride in the country. My mates were pea-green with jealousy.

All was going really well; it was a beautiful day, there was no real hurry, and my Four Hundred Four was purring like a kitten. My only problem was all the bugs splattering themselves across my visor. By the time I delivered my last parcel in Guildford, it was so full of them that I couldn't see through it. I had to ride with it flipped up, which I didn't mind, it being such a lovely day. A nice cooling breeze flowing around my face was just what the doctor ordered.

It was gone half-past four when I found a phone box to call in empty.

"You might as well slide on home from there," the controller said.

"I haven't collected my wages yet," I replied.

"Well you'd better get your skates on and hurry back then. The accounts office closes at half-five. Do you reckon you can make it in time?"

I looked at my watch and did a quick calculation. "Yeah, I can make it."

"You'll be squeezing it a bit tight, won't you?"

"Of course not; this is me you're talking to."

The controller laughed. "All right then Barry Sheene, I'll tell the accounts office to expect you."

I hung-up the phone and ran to the bike. No way was I going to miss out on my wages – there would have been hell to pay if I'd gone home without them. The bike howled away from the line and the race was on. As I scorched around the tight left-hander of the A3's slip-road, the speedo was nudging seventy and the left-hand footrest was skimming the tarmac.

Barry Sheene? I scoffed. *Bloody slow-coach compared to me, mate.*

Then, with a closing speed that felt like a hundred miles-an-hour, a kamikaze fly smashed into my left eye. For a split second I lost concentration; just a split second but that was enough. When I came to my senses, I found that I'd lost my line. I wasn't going to have enough room to make the bend. *No problem; shift your weight a bit and ease her over just a fraction more.* Of course, I could have backed the throttle off a bit but that was out of the question; I was a man on a mission!

I tried so hard, I should have made it. But unfortunately, even the mighty three-three was still bound by the laws of physics. The centre-stand lug hit the deck too hard and lifted the back wheel enough for the rear tyre to let go and down went the bike. Damn you gravity; damn you to hell!

The poor old girl slid through the Armco barrier, wiped out the alternator cover (I had a habit of wrecking those it seems) and bent the left handlebar almost in half! She looked so forlorn resting half in and half out of that indignant gorse bush.

Fortunately, I didn't have to slide too far before I also hit the Armco; but obviously, sliding for so short a distance meant I didn't have time to slow down any before I collided with it. I hit it hard enough to knock me spark out and I was out for so long that I didn't wake up until there was a policeman and an ambulance man looking down at me. This was the second time I'd been carried off in a meat-wagon in less than a year!

Now I say that hitting the Armco so quickly was fortunate simply because even having slid for such a short distance, I'd worn the skin on my left arm and leg away almost to the muscle. Gawd knows what sort of mess those limbs would have been in if I'd slid all the way to a stop!

Now if only I'd been wearing armour-plated, Kevlar-reinforced bike gear...

15: LOOKING BACK

I have a lot of memories of my time as a motorcycle messenger, and this book contains only a very few of them. Some, but not many, I remember rather fondly. Others, are remembrances of something that had to be endured. But there are other memories that I would rather forget; things that no matter how successful I am at putting them out of my mind, they always manage to make themselves known in my nightmares. Many times, I've woken up screaming with terror – not always from bike-related dreams, but mostly so.

It's funny, there are some things that at the time, I seemed to just laugh off – things that would have left many people in deep shock. I prided myself on being able to shrug off the several-times-a-day that I was nearly killed.

Whenever it rained, for a while the London streets became a greasy, slippery terror. But *only* for a while. The oily, rainbow coated muck would quickly be washed down the drains leaving the surface, if not grippy, at least negotiable.

One particular near-death incident occurred one horribly dreary morning as I was travelling along the Commercial Road. It was raining of sorts; but it was that nasty, fine, damp kind of rain that wasn't heavy enough to wash away the oil. Instead, it turned the roads into something more akin to an ice rink.

Gingerly, I eased my way along, not daring to overtake or even to try and filter between the snail-like lines of traffic. Fortunately, rush-hour was over and the wide Commercial Road was now relatively clear. I was following a Ford Capri, carefully giving myself the luxury of plenty of stopping distance. When we came up to a red light, I didn't move alongside him ready for the usual traffic-light Grand Prix. There was no point, if I'd given the bike the beans, the back wheel would have just spun impotently, and he would have easily beaten me away from the line.

So there I was, sitting behind the car, merrily humming a tune to myself – usually a Meatloaf track – when my 'radar' made me look into my mirror. To my horror, a large coach was bearing down on me at a rate of knots with its wheels locked up completely. I was clearly about to be squashed as flat as the proverbial pancake. With lightning reflexes, I stamped the bike into first gear. I knew I had to be careful not to spin the rear wheel, so with laudable presence of mind, I fed in the clutch as swiftly but as gently as I could.

The coach must have missed the back of my bike by mere millimetres as it smashed into the back of the unfortunate Capri. I swear it must have been doing a good 40 mph because the car was sent careering all the way across the junction to the other side of the lights. Its back end was crushed beyond all recognition and the vehicle was obviously a write-off. I had no time to hang around, and as there were plenty of witnesses, I continued on my way.

I thought nothing of it other than it being a good tale to tell my mates. Sometimes, I managed to get 'parked-up' with a lot of other riders. And as it was such a tight-knit community, even if you didn't know any of the others there, you'd soon be chatting away as though you'd been friends for years. Our conversation was almost always full of laughter as we swapped such death-defying tales of derring-do. Even when we were bitching about our lot in life, the deep fellowship we felt mitigated our woes. Little did I know how often those laughed-at experiences would resurface so many years later.

I'm not making a big deal out of it though; there are many, many others from all walks of life with just as much mental baggage – and many with much more.

There were at least some benefits as well as misery to the life of a despatch rider. Would you believe that I've owned or leased more than sixty bikes? Riding them, I've managed to clock up over half a million miles on two wheels. And these bikes range from 50cc mopeds (proper sports mopeds, not today's emasculated, 30 mph, twist-and-go monstrosities) to fire breathing muscle bikes. Strangely, some of my favourite bolides for slicing around the capital's overcrowded streets were small bikes. Things like the diminutive but surprisingly useful Honda CB250RS. I've also got a particularly soft spot for the humble 200 Benly. For such a simple, boring commuter, it was amazingly agile, quick, reliable, frugal, and easy to service. If it was a busy period and I wanted to stay local and carry lots of jobs at once, this was the kiddie for me. The trade-off came when the work dropped away. Then, it was the long jobs that made up your wages, and this poor wee beastie – as willing as it was – was totally out of its depth on the motorway. An 80mph top whack equates to a realistic 65mph cruising speed.

In spite of the motorway drawbacks, I never stopped singing the wee Honda's praises to any that would listen – I even wrote a poem about it.

Oh Benly, oh Benly you've stolen my heart,
Even though your exhaust note sounds like a wet fart.
Your handling is dodgy, your brakes are a scare,

Your engine is gutless, but I just don't care.
There's no other bike for which my heart doth clamour,
But I'm trading you in for a five-hundred Gamma!

Another one of the benefits of the life (and it was a *lifestyle* rather than just a job) was the number of celebrities I met. One or two of them I became quite friendly with. One of them (I won't embarrass the poor man by naming him but he is connected with the words 'house', 'adder', and 'fry') even handed me the keys to his brand spanking new Moto-Guzzi. "Here, have a go," he said cheerily. I've recently tried reaching out to him for a chat but to no avail. He probably doesn't even remember me.

Most of the celebrities I met were those I either delivered to or collected from. Damon Hill even rode for the same despatch company as me once. I wonder if he remembers any of his old comrades at arms. I wouldn't be surprised, he knew a few of them a lot better than me and he was (is?) a genuinely decent man.

I *almost* met Rory Mcgrath once. It was a really quiet summer's day and a few of my friends and I were on stand-by in Broadwick Street, Soho. There was a nice little café there with a continental feel to it. We all ordered a coffee and sat at one of the pavement tables in the sunshine.

As usual, we were swapping tales, taking the piss out of each other and generally engaging in our riotously funny banter. As the minutes passed, I noticed a chap on the table next to us. He was with a couple of others but was paying no attention to their conversation. Instead, he was leaning towards us, listening to our comic antics with a faint but intrigued smile playing on his lips.

All I can say, Rory who-I-almost-met, is that I'm genuinely pleased we entertained you that summer's afternoon in Broadwick Street. And don't worry, I won't be claiming breach of copyright if you managed to use any of the material you gleaned from us poor, downtrodden bikers that day.

So, there it is, dear reader. A tiny glimpse into the past. It was actually a fantastic time to be a biker. Technology was beginning to take huge leaps forward (and sideways with the ridiculously stupid turbo models). It was all new, exciting, and fresh. Best of all, speed cameras were not yet even a glint in PC Plod's avaricious eye. Ah yes, halcyon days indeed. Shame they were spoilt by having no choice but to ride all day, every working day. No choice but to face rain, maiming, sleet, death, ice, death, snow, *death*, fog, DEATH, freezing fog...

Nurse! Where's my tablets?

Printed in Great Britain
by Amazon

79929742R00079